COLOR
INSIDE
THE LINES

©2015 Brandon Hayes

All rights reserved. No part of this publication may be reproduced or transmitted in any form or by any means, electronic or mechanical, including photocopy, recording or any information storage and retrieval system, without permission in writing from the author. For information regarding permission, write Brandon Hayes at brandonhayesart@gmail.com

ISBN 13: 978-1517653125
WWW.BRANDONHAYESART.COM
INSTAGRAM: @BRANDON_HAYES_ART

For my wife, Lara, my rock, without you I would be adrift in the world. I love you!
For my children, Noel and Jack, for making me laugh every day. I love you two!
To Rachael, for giving me the push.
And to everyone else who has helped me along the way. Thank you!

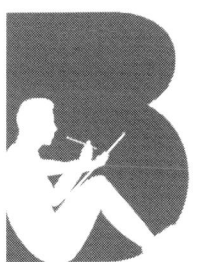

Welcome to my black and white world on a trip through fantasy Asia.

Take yourself back to childhood and get lost in this magical land I have created. Travel through mountains, along streams, meeting dragons and exotic birds. Along with your trusty guide, a Very Sharp colored pencil (my personal favorite), help me bring these scenes to life. Remember to have fun and never forget to feed your inner child.
ENJOY!

SHARE YOUR COLORING WITH ME!
Use the hashtag #BHColorInsideTheLines

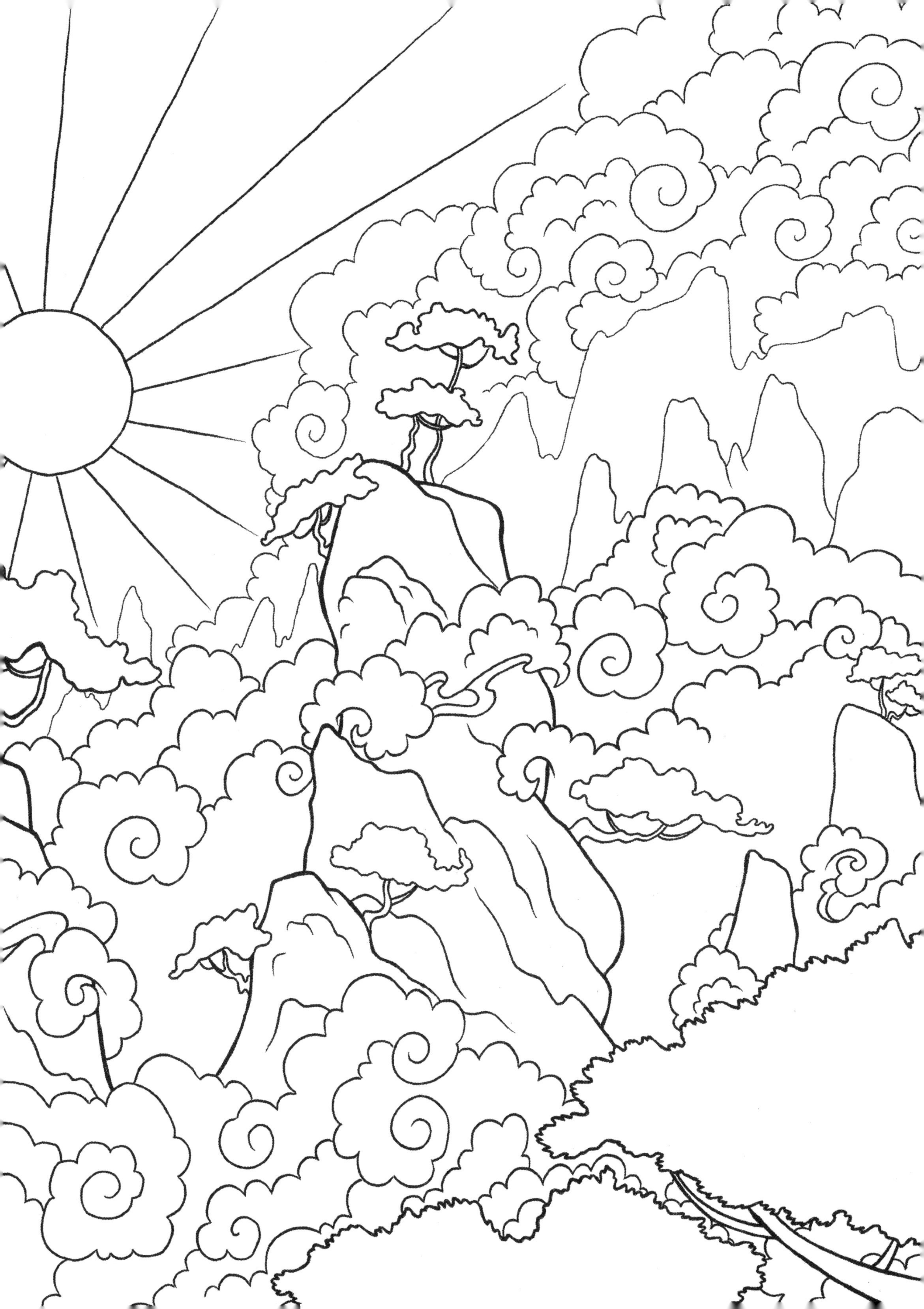

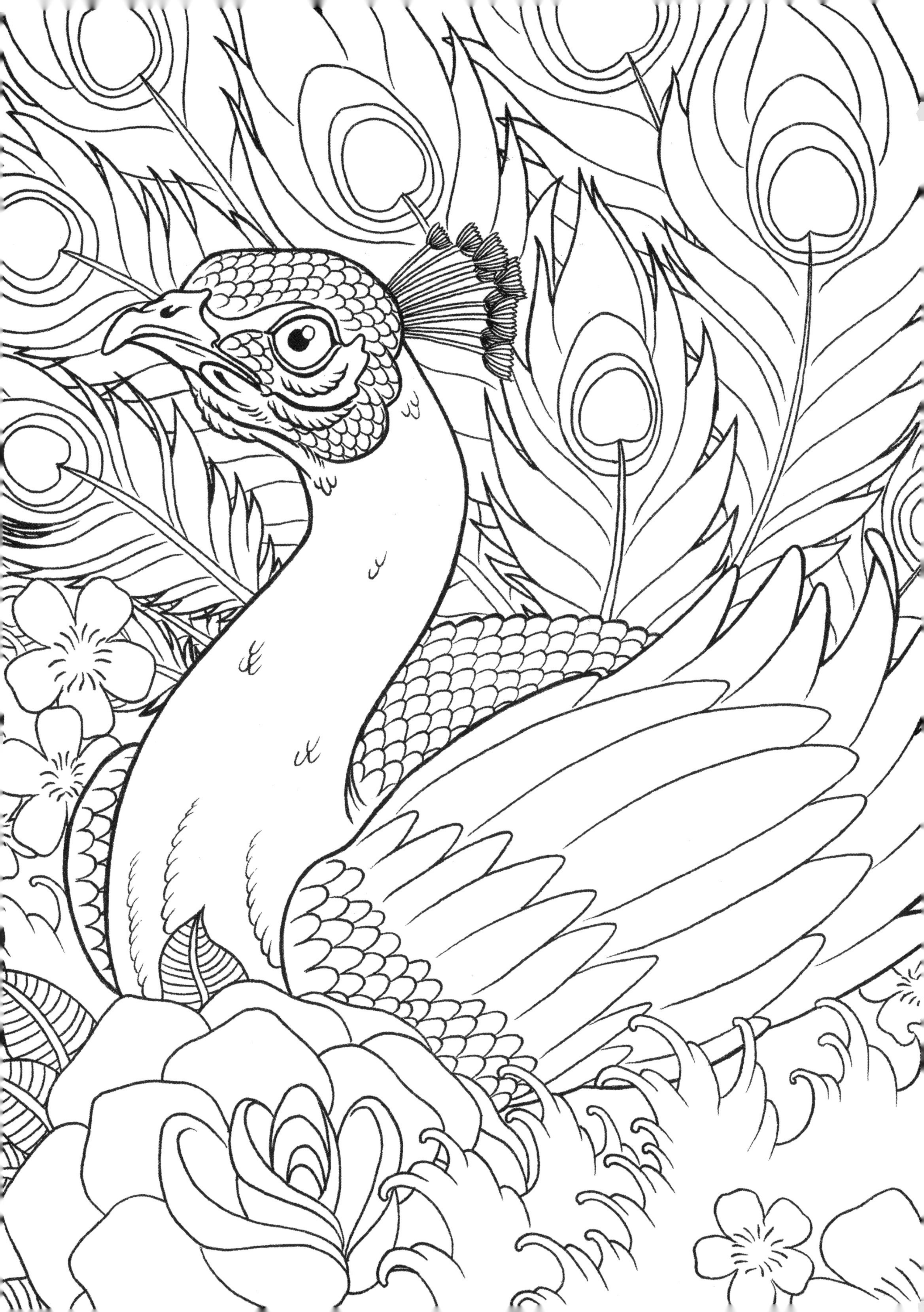

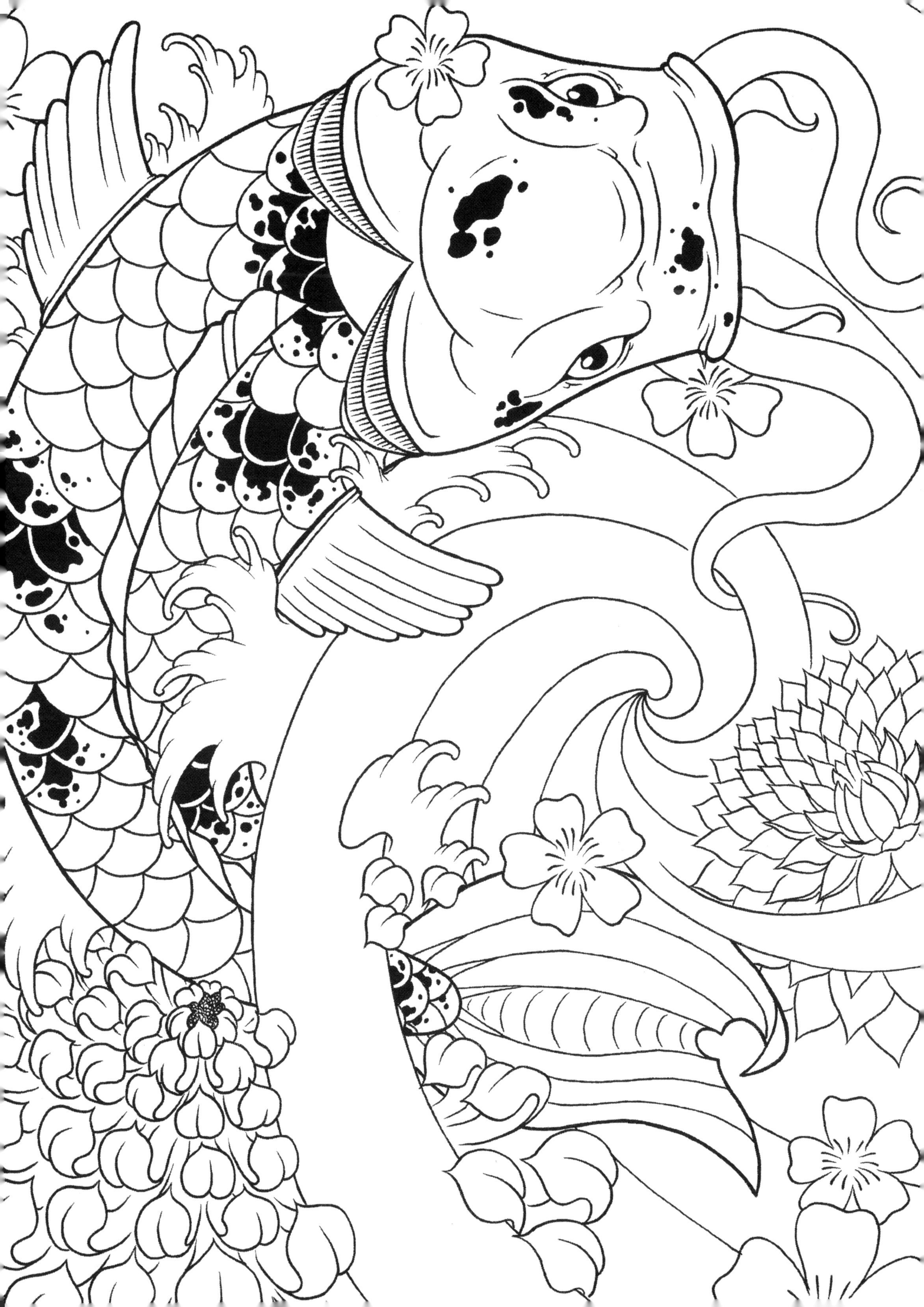

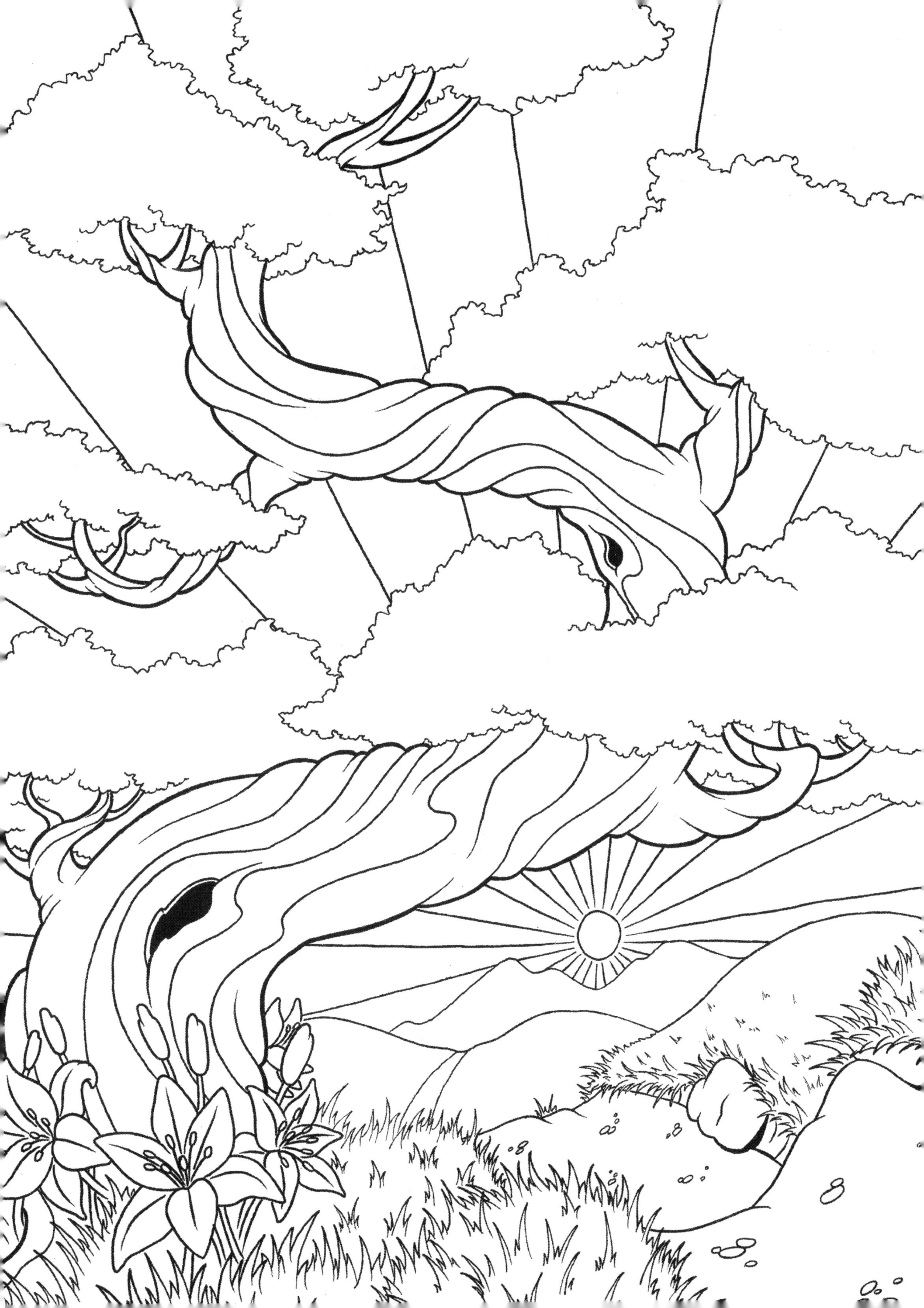

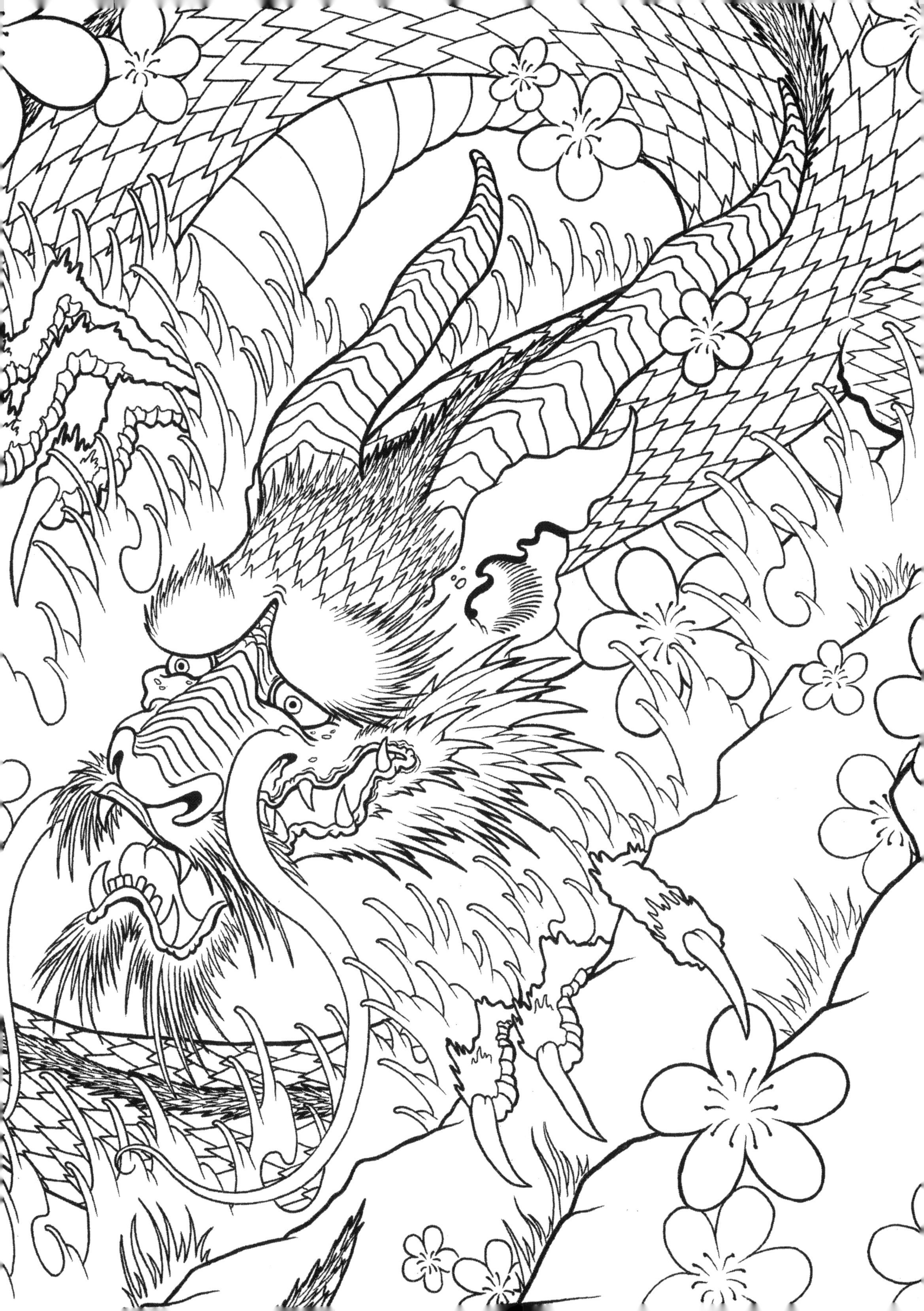

Made in the USA
Middletown, DE
02 April 2016